Sendak at the Rosenbach

An exhibition held at the Rosenbach Museum & Library
April 28–October 30, 1995

Vincent Giroud and Maurice Sendak, *Curators*

FRONT COVER
32
Mahler. Illustration for cover of RCA recording
of his Third Symphony, 1976.

BACK COVER
34
Really Rosie, poster for the New York production, 1980.

Library of Congress Catalog Card Number: 95-68402

ISBN 0-939084-27-9

Photography	Robert Lisak and Studio Lux
Design	Greer Allen
Typesetting	Highwood Typographic Services in Baskerville text and Bookman display using QuarkXpress
Printing	Thames Printing Company, Inc.
Binding	Mueller Trade Bindery

PRINTED IN THE UNITED STATES OF AMERICA

*This exhibition and catalogue
are dedicated to the memory of Jack Sendak, the artist's brother*

24
Samuel Palmer.
"The Lonely Tower."

4
Illustration for pages 26–27
of *The Moon Jumpers*, 1959.

Foreword

In a lifetime of making and illustrating books, Maurice Sendak has contributed to American literature an astonishing body of creative work. In a lifetime of collecting, he has assembled exceptional examples of literature and art that the careful observer can often find reflected in Sendak's creative efforts. Sendak's passion for books and his inability to resist a new find would have made him an ideal client of A.S.W. Rosenbach, the great book dealer who, with his brother Philip, established this museum. Sendak and Rosenbach would have been friends too: Rosenbach's first personal collection was the unprecedented group of early American children's books now at the Free Library of Philadelphia. Rosenbach would have marveled at the range of Sendak's work, from the early, brash illustrations for *Atomics for the Millions* to the recent seductive, Blake-influenced watercolors for Melville's *Pierre*. Rosenbach would have delighted in the richness of imagery and imagination in picture books such as *Where the Wild Things Are* and *In the Night Kitchen*. In their common passion for books, these two bibliophiles would have found a universe of shared pleasure.

The Rosenbach that Maurice Sendak first visited in the late 1960s was a different place from what it is today. Maurice recalls settling into the late Philip Rosenbach's bed, a first edition Melville in his hands and Philip's fur coverlet warming him. Since then, the Rosenbach has restricted collections research to the reading room. Unfortunately for the staff, the beds are now all gone. What continues unaltered, however, is the Rosenbach's fundamental commitment to the printed page. At a time when the average American teenager spends eighteen hours watching television each week but less than two hours reading, the Rosenbach has a special mandate to promote books as the historical core of learning. While Maurice Sendak as a creator and collector of books is the subject of this exhibition, *Sendak at the Rosenbach* also celebrates the central, continuing importance of the printed page as the primary conveyor of Western culture.

Sendak at the Rosenbach, the last of three exhibitions in the Rosenbach's 40th Anniversary Exhibition Program, has been made possible by the generosity of our members and by special gifts from William M. Hollis, Jr. and Andrea M. Baldeck, M.D., the Quaker Chemical Foundation, the Berwind Corporation, the Richardson Company, the Institute of Museum Services (a federal agency), the Pennsylvania Council on the Arts, and the Philadelphia Cultural Fund. The exhibition is part of *Sendak in Philadelphia*, a collaboration with the Please Touch Museum®, which has installed a permanent, interactive exhibition for children based on Sendak's books. Our collaboration received assistance from HarperCollins Publishers, the CIGNA Foundation, the Independence Foundation, the Foundation for New Era Philanthropy, and PECO Energy Company. A generous grant from the Connelly Foundation and gifts from Sylvan Barnet and Anne Gates Yarnall funded publication of this catalogue. We are grateful for the support of all of these friends.

The Rosenbach also appreciates the collegiality of Ralph Franklin, director of Yale University's Beinecke Rare Book and Manuscript Library, in allowing Vincent Giroud, its curator of modern books and manuscripts, to serve as guest co-curator of this exhibition. Maurice Sendak and Vincent Giroud worked together in all stages of the exhibition, and I thank both of them for bringing equal measures of brilliance and good humor to the project. Thanks are also due to Christa Sammons, curator of German literature at the Beinecke Library, for her editorial assistance. Finally, I thank Nancy Kolb, president and executive director of the Please Touch Museum®, for hatching with me the unlikeliest collaboration that the Philadelphia museum community could have imagined.

STEPHEN K. URICE, *Director*

11
Illustration for page 15
of *The Golden Key*, 1967.

Introduction

This exhibition presents forty-three years of book illustrating, from 1952 to 1995, and nearly as many years of collecting. It also documents fifteen years of a new career, beginning in 1980, as set and costume designer in opera and the music theater.

The purpose of this juxtaposition is to show how closely the creativity of the illustrator and the interests of the collector are interrelated. Over the years, the collector has gathered first or early editions, engravings, and original artwork by the writers and artists who appeal most to the illustrator's imagination and who have most influenced his work. It is our hope that the visitor will recognize George Cruikshank in the Ruth Krauss and Little Bear books, Arthur Hughes and George Pinwell in *Higglety Pigglety Pop!* and the George MacDonald books, Rowlandson and Caldecott in *The Bee-Man of Orn,* Ludwig Grimm in *The Juniper Tree,* and, most admired and most present of all, William Blake, from *Charlotte and the White Horse* and *Lullabies and Night Songs* to the newly conceived illustrations to Herman Melville's *Pierre.*

These many, diverse influences account to a large extent for the diversity of the books themselves. While the visitor will immediately identify a number of recurrent themes or stylistic traits, he or she will be equally struck by the contrast, say, between the worlds of *Zlateh the Goat* and *In the Night Kitchen,* or those of *Fly by Night* and *Outside Over There.* One reason is that the illustrator is self-trained; he grew and evolved with each new book (even though some of the early ones remain favorites). Another, more profound reason is that the illustrator is more interested in immersing himself in the personality of each book than in achieving a unique, consistent, personal illustrative style from one book to the next.

Illustrated books, and this is especially true of children's books, fall into two categories, the story book and the picture book. The story book illustrator is bound by the constraints of the text he is illustrating: Frank Stockton, George MacDonald, Randall Jarrell, Isaac Bashevis Singer, the Brothers Grimm, and Herman Melville each demand a specific, appropriate style of illustration. The artist hopes that his illustrations will add something to the text (as Tenniel's have done so memorably to Lewis Carroll's *Alice*) but they are nevertheless bound by it. The picture book has no such constraints, or rather it only has its own internal constraints. The text and images of *Where the Wild Things Are, In the Night Kitchen,* and *Outside Over There,* conceived together, are inseparable from each other. They are fused in the same way as an opera's libretto and its music. In fact, this artist views the creation of a picture book as closely related to musical composition and believes that the greatest examples of the genre achieve a quasi-musical rhythm and vitality that are spontaneously perceived as such by their readers.

This analogy will perhaps help to understand why the book illustrator, for whom music has always been the chief source of inspiration, underwent a career change in the 1980s to devote himself almost entirely to the world of opera and the music theater, especially opera and music theater for children, and why this should be seen less as a change than a continuation.

VINCENT GIROUD
MAURICE SENDAK

Catalogue

I
Books by Maurice Sendak

1 A Hole Is to Dig

Ruth Krauss. *A Hole Is to Dig: A First Book of First Definitions.* Pictures by Maurice Sendak. New York: Harper & Brothers, 1952.

Sendak met Ruth Krauss, by then an established author of children's books, via Ursula Nordstrom, his mentor and editor at Harper & Brothers. A Hole Is to Dig, *their first collaboration, established his own reputation. Originally printed on brown-tinted paper, it is a series of definitions reflecting childlike logic (many supplied by children themselves), each illustrated by a lively scene, such as a dog-kissing party or a collective mud-bath. Krauss and her husband, the writer, painter, and cartoonist Crockett Johnson, lived in Rowayton, Connecticut and they and Sendak became lifelong friends. Seven more books with Ruth Krauss appeared between 1953 and 1960:* A Very Special House, I'll Be You and You Be Me, Charlotte and the White Horse, I Want to Paint My Bathroom Blue, The Birthday Party, Somebody Else's Nut Tree and Other Tales from Children, *and* Open House for Butterflies. *Ruth Krauss died in 1994.*

2 Little Bear

Else Holmelund Minarik. *Little Bear.* Pictures by Maurice Sendak. New York: Harper & Brothers, 1957. (An "I Can Read" Book.)

Like Ruth Krauss, Else Minarik became a close friend. Following the success of Little Bear, *her first book, she and Sendak produced five more books:* No Fighting, No Biting! *(1958),* Father Bear Comes Home *(1959),* Little Bear's Friend *(1960),* Little Bear's Visit *(1961), and* A Kiss for Little Bear *(1968). Written for first-grade apprentice-readers, the Little Bear series was illustrated by Sendak in a style looking back to the Victorian era, as evidenced both by the dress worn by his animal heroes and his characteristic use of crosshatching in the manner of George Cruikshank.*

3 What Do You...?

Sesyle Joslin. *What Do You Do, Dear? Proper Conduct for All Occasions.* Pictures by Maurice Sendak. New York: William R. Scott, 1961. (Young Scott Books)

This is the second of Sesyle Joslin's two playful parodies of etiquette manuals for children, following What Do You Say, Dear?, *published in 1958. Both are organized around a series of questions and answers, each featuring a more outlandish situation than the other, with an endearingly mischievous pair of children cast in the various roles. The most dramatic scene (which serves as cover illustration) features a boy pilot—a forerunner of Mickey the aviator of* In the Night Kitchen—*faced with the following situation: "You are flying around in your airplane and you remember that the Duchess said, 'Do drop in for tea sometime.'" Upon which he crashes his plane through the ceiling of the girl duchess's room, while the bemused dog (Sendak's own Jennie), suspended on the chandelier, stares at the apologetic intruder.*

4 The Moon Jumpers

Janice May Udry. *The Moon Jumpers.* Pictures by Maurice Sendak. New York: Harper & Brothers, 1959.

Original pen-and-ink and watercolor dummy, dated December 15, 1957.

Original tempera drawing for pages 26–27.

Janice May Udry's simple tale involves four children playing outside on a summer evening. Purple, dark green, and blue dominate in the full-color illustrations. The theme of the book, which culminates in a full-page wild dance to the moon, and its illustrative style both anticipate the "rumpus" of Where the Wild Things Are.

5 Mr. Rabbit

Charlotte Zolotow. *Mr. Rabbit and the Lovely Present.* Pictures by Maurice Sendak. New York and Evanston: Harper & Brothers, 1962.

"Mr. Rabbit and the Little Girl": original pen-and-ink and watercolor dummy, n.d.

Original watercolor drawing for page 13.

Sendak spent the summer of 1961 in Vergennes, Vermont, and this setting inspired his colorful illustrations for Charlotte Zolotow's tale of a little girl whose search for a present for her mother is guided by a friendly rabbit. The delicate blues and greens of its palette owe much to the watercolors of Winslow Homer.

5
Illustration for page 13
of *Mr. Rabbitt and the Lovely Present*, 1962.

6 The Griffin and the Minor Canon

Frank R. Stockton. *The Griffin and the Minor Canon.* Illustrations by Maurice Sendak. New York, Chicago, San Francisco: Holt, Rinehart and Winston, 1963.

Unbound preliminary dummy book with original pen-and-ink and watercolor drawing, n.d.

Once one of the best-loved American authors of fiction for children, the Philadelphia-born Frank Stockton (1834–1902), originally trained as an engraver, contributed many short stories to St. Nicholas Magazine *between 1873 and 1881. His delightful tale of a griffin coming to a small town to contemplate his sculpted effigy on the cathedral porch and the community's cruelty towards their quietly heroic, childlike canon is accompanied by sharply outlined black-and-white illustrations; the crosshatching and limited coloring contribute to the period-piece character of the book.*

7 Where the Wild Things Are

Where the Wild Things Are. Story and Pictures by Maurice Sendak. New York: Harper & Row, 1963.

"Where the Wild Horses Are": oblong original pen and watercolor dummy, dated November 17, 1955.

Original pen and watercolor dummy for *Where the Wild Things Are*, dated May 25, 1963.

"Version I: Where the Wild Things are": holograph manuscript, May 10, 1963.

Original pen-and-ink line and watercolor drawing for page [15].

Original pen-and-ink and watercolor drawing for pages [22–23].

Original pen-and-ink line and watercolor drawing for pages [26–27].

The eighth of the books both written and illustrated by Sendak, Where the Wild Things Are *remains to this day his best known and most popular. It is also his first genuine "picture book," that is to say a book in which the images and text perfectly blend. Its inception goes back to 1955, when Sendak projected a picture book entitled "Where the Wild Horses Are." Having convinced himself that he could not draw horses, he came up with a personal fantasy in which the horses became half-human, half-animal "things," monstrous—yet affectionate—impersonations of his half-feared, half-detested relatives as remembered from his Brooklyn childhood. Max, the hero, is thus both a personal projection (and Jennie, Sendak's beloved Sealyham, duly appears in the story) and an archetypal figure of the rebellious child, with whom millions of young readers have enthusiastically identified since the book's appearance. Inspired in part by William Nicholson's* The Pirate Twins *(1929), it also evokes* L'enfant et les sortilèges, *the 1925 opera by Colette and Maurice Ravel, which Sendak later designed at Glyndebourne. An immediate, immense, if not totally uncontroversial success,* Where the Wild Things Are *was awarded the Caldecott Medal in 1964. It has been translated into more than fifteen languages worldwide.*

8 The Bee-Man of Orn

Frank R. Stockton. *The Bee-Man of Orn.* Pictures by Maurice Sendak. New York, Chicago, San Francisco: Holt, Rinehart and Winston, 1964.

Original pen-and-ink and watercolor drawing for pages 36–37.

Like The Griffin and the Minor Canon, The Bee-Man of Orn *was written for* St. Nicholas Magazine, *where it appeared in November 1883. The illustrations pay tribute to two English artists much admired by Sendak: Randolph Caldecott, the great 19th-century children's book illustrator, and the caricaturist Thomas Rowlandson.*

8
The Bee-Man of Orn, 1964.
Title page and illustration for pages 36–37.

6
The Griffin and the Minor Canon, 1963. Dummy.

9 The Bat-Poet

Randall Jarrell. *The Bat-Poet*. Pictures by Maurice Sendak. New York: The Macmillan Company; London: Collier-Macmillan Limited, 1964.

Original pen-and-ink drawing for page 1.

The Nashville-born poet, novelist, critic, and translator Randall Jarrell (1914–65) was also the author of several books for children, three of which were published with illustrations by Sendak. This is the tale of a bat who instead of sleeping in the daytime observes the world and writes poems, which he recites to the other animals (and which form part of the book). Here, Sendak uses a style of minutely crosshatched drawings which could almost be confused with engravings, giving the book a classical, harmonious look.

10 Zlateh the Goat

Isaac Bashevis Singer. *Zlateh the Goat and Other Stories*. Translated from the Yiddish by the author and Elizabeth Shub. Pictures by Maurice Sendak. New York: Harper & Row, 1966. No. 9 from a limited edition of 500 copies on Andorra paper, specially bound and numbered, and signed by the author and artist.

Original pen-and-ink drawing for page 28.

Originally called The Devil's Trick and Other Stories, *this collection of seven folkloric tales of the shtetl by the 1978 winner of the Nobel Prize for literature takes its new title from the last and most moving story, which tells of a boy lost in the snow with a goat. In his foreword, Singer characterizes the book as a memorial to a lost world and dedicates it to the children who died victims of the Holocaust. In his own parallel fashion, Sendak made it a memorial to his Old Country relatives who perished at Auschwitz by using their faces, drawn from old photographs, in several of his illustrations. His pen-and-ink drawings, strongly suggestive of etchings, add a touchingly human dimension to Singer's deliberately dry, unemotional prose.*

9
Cover jacket and illustration for page 1 of *The Bat-Poet*, 1964.

10
Zlateh the Goat, 1966.
Illustration for page 28 and opening page of "The First Schlemiel."

BOOKS BY SENDAK *13*

7
Illustrations for page [15], *above*, and *opposite* for pages [22–23] and [26–27] of *Where the Wild Things Are*, 1963.

11 The Golden Key

George MacDonald. *The Golden Key.* With Pictures by Maurice Sendak. Afterword by W.H. Auden. New York: Farrar, Straus and Giroux, 1967. (An Ariel Book)

Original pen-and-ink drawing for page 15.

Together with his better-known contemporary and friend Lewis Carroll, George MacDonald (1824–1905) was among the greatest Victorian writers for children. A Congregationalist minister, he was himself the father of eleven children and his stories were intended for them. Such is the case with "The Golden Key," which was first published in the collection Dealings with the Fairies *in 1867, with illustrations by Arthur Hughes. It is the story of two children: the girl is called Tangle because of her messy hair, the boy Mossy on account of his habit of sitting with a book on a stone covered with moss. As the tale progresses, they grow older, get separated, to be finally reunited at the end of the book, which is also the end of their lives. To this enigmatic, allegorical tale, Sendak responded with pen-and-ink illustrations in the style of the period, which capture its haunting atmosphere. For one of its most memorable images, showing Tangle delivered by the air-fish from the branches of a tree which is entrapping her, he gave his heroine the features of Irene MacDonald, one of the author's children, from a photograph by Lewis Carroll.*

12 Higglety Pigglety Pop!

Higglety Pigglety Pop! Or, There Must Be More to Life. Story and Pictures by Maurice Sendak. New York: Harper & Row, 1967.

Original pen-and-ink drawings for pages 54, 55, and 56.

Jennie, Sendak's beloved companion since 1953, died in 1967 after developing cancer. She had appeared in most of his books beside Where the Wild Things Are. Higglety Pigglety Pop!, *of which she is fully the heroine, is an affectionate portrait and a farewell. It is also the longest of Sendak's own tales. Jennie leaves her master, and after taming an ill-tempered baby to whom Sendak lent his own former features, she becomes the star of the World Mother Goose Theater. The play in which she performs, "Higglety Pigglety Pop!," interrupts the tale and forms the illustrative core of the book. Its title—and text—are taken from a nonsense rhyme written in 1846 by Samuel Griswold Goodrich, author of the children's classic Peter Parley tales, and a native of Ridgefield, Connecticut, where Sendak was to settle in 1972. The illustrations, a number of which were drawn from actual photographs of Jennie, bear witness once again to Sendak's love for the great Victorian illustrators, especially Arthur Hughes and George Pinwell.*

12
Illustrations for pages 54, 55, and 56 of *Higglety Pigglety Pop!*, 1967.

11
The Golden Key, 1967.

13 The Light Princess

George MacDonald. *The Light Princess*. With Pictures by Maurice Sendak. New York: Farrar, Straus and Giroux, 1969. (An Ariel Book)

Original pen-and-ink drawing for page 101.

The second George MacDonald book Sendak illustrated (a third one, The Portent, *followed in 1979) originally appeared as part of* Adela Cathcart *in 1864 and was reprinted three years later in* Dealings with the Fairies. *It is the tale, in turn witty and moving, of a princess who has been deprived of her gravity by a wicked aunt who was not invited to her christening. The princess is also "light" in a metaphorical sense, being incapable of seriousness. The story shows her gradual awakening to love, culminating in the dramatic scene in which she has to rescue, through her own will, the prince who is about to drown for her sake.*

14 In the Night Kitchen

In the Night Kitchen. New York: Harper & Row, 1970.

Original ink line drawing for pages [8–9]

Original watercolor illustration with line transparency for half-title.

Original watercolor drawing with acetate overlay for pages [28–29]

In the Night Kitchen *was born of an abortive project of an illustrated Mother Goose, irrepressibly centered on the themes of food and eating. What developed instead was a dream book, conceived as a literal illustration of the Sunshine Bakers advertisement: "We Bake While You Sleep!" Its hero was named Mickey after Walt Disney's creation—a near-contemporary of Sendak, himself an ardent collector of Mickey Mousiana. The illustrative style of* In the Night Kitchen *owes much to early newspaper comics such as Winsor McCay's* Little Nemo in Slumberland *(1905–11), while the Oliver Hardy likeness of the three bakers is a tribute to the prewar comic films. Dedicated to Sendak's parents, it is the most autobiographical of his picture books, full of personal references such as the clock memorializing Jennie. The success of the book was in part a succès de scandale, caused mainly by Mickey's frontal nudity, which prompted some librarians to add a painted-on diaper to the picture. In an editorial entitled "Sex, Drugs and Sendak," published on 1 October 1994, the* New York Times *columnist Anna Quindlen, citing examples in Beloit, Wisconsin, Norridge, Illinois, and Elk River, Minnesota, reminded one that these puritanical reactions are still in force.*

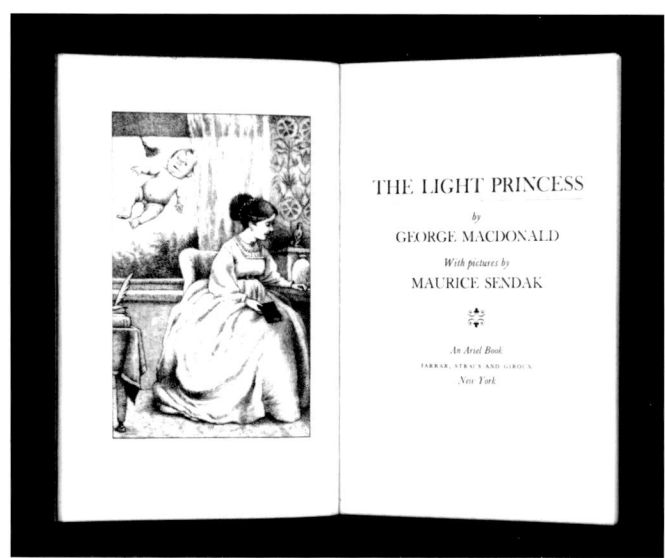

13
The Light Princess, 1969.
Title page with frontispiece
and, *opposite*, illustration for page 101.

14
In the Night Kitchen, 1970.

15
The Juniper Tree, 1973. "The Goblins," frontispiece illustration for vol. 1.; *opposite above*, illustration for "Hansel and Gretel;" *opposite below*, illustration for "The Devil and His Three Golden Hairs."

15 The Juniper Tree

Wilhelm Grimm. *The Juniper Tree and Other Tales from Grimm*. Selected by Lore Segal and Maurice Sendak. Translated by Lore Segal. With four tales translated by Randall Jarrell. Pictures by Maurice Sendak. New York: Farrar, Straus and Giroux, 1973. Two volumes.

"There suddenly came a lot of little goblins": original pen-and-ink drawing for "The Goblins," frontispiece to volume 1.

"Oh, how the poor little sister did grieve!": original pen-and-ink drawing for "Hansel and Gretel."

An illustrated anthology of tales by the Brothers Grimm had been planned with Randall Jarrell, who in 1962 had published translations of five of them. Brought to a halt by Jarrell's untimely death in 1965, the project was resurrected by Michael di Capua when he joined Farrar, Straus & Giroux as an editor; 27 tales were selected, four in Jarrell's translations (including "Hansel and Gretel" and "Snow White and the Seven Dwarfs"), the rest translated by the Austrian-born novelist and children's book writer Lore Segal. Published in two volumes, the selection, titled after one of the most hauntingly beautiful of the Grimm Brothers' tales, sums up in unbowdlerized form the macabre and cruel world of the original. For his illustrations—27 drawings, one for each tale, including the two frontispieces—Sendak had prepared himself by travelling to Germany in 1971. Grünewald and Dürer are two strong influences (the size of the drawings is that of the latter's Little Passion); so are some of the tales' earliest illustrators, notably Ludwig Grimm and George Cruikshank. This monumental edition has been recognized as Sendak's masterpiece as a story-book illustrator.

17
Illustrations for pages [22–23] and [34–35]
of *Outside Over There*, 1981.

19
Illustrations for pages [4–5] and [26–27]
of *We Are All in the Dumps with Jack and Guy*, 1993.

16 Fly by Night

Randall Jarrell. *Fly by Night.* Pictures by Maurice Sendak. New York: Farrar, Straus & Giroux, 1976.

Original pen-and-ink drawing for pages 26–27.

Completed by Jarrell shortly before his death, Fly by Night *is the story of a boy named David who lives in a house at the edge of the forest and floats in the air during the night. Like* The Bat-Poet, *which was interspersed with poetry, the tale leads to a long poem. "The Owl's Bedtime Story" is immediately followed by a double-page illustration in which Sendak included an image of himself as a baby in his mother's arms, as well as another, younger image of his mother as a shepherdess, drawn from old family photographs.*

17 Outside Over There

Outside Over There. New York: Harper & Row, 1981.

Original watercolor drawing for pages [22–23], dated August 25, 1978.

Preliminary study for the jacket: pencil drawing on tracing paper, dated April 15, 1979.

Original watercolor drawing for pages [34–35], dated January 1979.

The Juniper Tree *includes a short, little-known tale entitled "The Goblins," the illustration to which serves as a frontispiece to the first volume of the anthology. "Once there was a mother and the goblins had stolen her child out of the cradle. In its place they laid a changeling with thick head and staring eyes who did nothing but eat and drink." This ghoulish tale of abduction combined itself in Sendak's imagination with terrified childhood memories of the kidnapping and subsequent death of the Lindbergh baby in March 1932. (His features are actually given to Ida's little sister in one of the illustrations, while Ida herself was drawn after a young girl named Esme.) The atmosphere of German Romanticism permeates the whole book, from Ida's "Wunderhorn" to references to the works of Philip Otto Runge and Caspar David Friedrich.* Outside Over There *forms, by Sendak's own admission, the final part of a picture-book trilogy, launched with* Where the Wild Things Are *and continued with* In the Night Kitchen. *Treated in a deliberately operatic mode, with strong Mozartian undertones, the book also heralds Sendak's new career as an opera designer.*

16
Fly by Night, 1976.
Book opening and illustration for pages 26–27.

17
Outside Over There, 1981.
Preliminary study and jacket.

18 Dear Mili

Wilhelm Grimm. *Dear Mili*. An old tale... newly translated by Ralph Manheim. With Pictures by Maurice Sendak. New York: Farrar, Straus and Giroux, 1988. (Published by Michael di Capua Books)

Rediscovered in September 1983, this story by Wilhelm Grimm was preserved in a letter he wrote to a little girl in 1816, which had remained in the possession of her family since that time. It is not difficult to see why the tale appealed to Sendak's creative imagination: like Outside Over There, *it deals with the disappearance of a child. It is a sombre tale, which unfolds against a background of war and death. Sendak's fifteen illustrations, three of them double pages, once again draw their inspiration from the German Romantics, notably Friedrich, while the giant flowers evoke the world of Carl Wilhelm Kolbe.*

19 We Are All in the Dumps

We Are All in the Dumps with Jack and Guy. Two Nursery Rhymes with Pictures by Maurice Sendak. New York: Harper Collins, 1993. (Michael di Capua Books)

Original pen-and-ink and watercolor drawings for pages [4–5] and [26–27].

Mother Goose rhymes have always been part of Sendak's world. In 1965, he had combined two of them, Hector Protector *and* As I Went over the Water, *into a picture book; and one of his major works,* Higglety Pigglety Pop! *is built on one. The story he grafts on the little-known "We Are All in the Dumps" and "Jack and Guy" is another tale of kidnapping and rescue. It is set in the desolate urban landscape of the slums of New York City (Brooklyn Bridge and the Trump Tower being two recognizable landmarks), with a cast of homeless children and abandoned cats, while the headlines of torn newspapers evoke the tragedies of homelessness, unemployment and AIDS, contrasting with the greed of the economically successful. The moon, which figured frequently in previous Sendak books (Where the Wild Things Are, for one), plays here a central role, in turn a distressed observer and a protective agent.* We Are All in the Dumps with Jack and Guy, *Sendak's pessimistic outlook on the situation of our modern inner cities, ends nevertheless on a note of hope: the two boys take charge of the baby and the three of them create a new family.*

20 Pierre

Herman Melville. *Pierre; or, The Ambiguities*. Illustrations by Maurice Sendak. (To be published by HarperCollins in September 1995)

Two preliminary pencil sketches on tracing paper.

Illustrating Melville's Pierre, *his favorite book by his favorite American novelist, is a project Sendak has long hoped to bring to fruition. His* Pierre *will be accompanied by 24 small vignettes in color, approximately of the size of Blake's engravings for* The Songs of Innocence *and* The Song of Experience *and are strongly influenced by Blake, the poet and artist Sendak venerates above all others.*

18
Dear Mili, 1988.

II
Sendak as a Collector

21 Blake

William Hayley. *Little Tom the Sailor.* Broadside with engraved poem and two relief etchings by William Blake. N.p., 5 October 1800.

From September 1800 until September 1803, Blake and his wife lived in Felpham, on the coast of Sussex, in a cottage rented from the philanthropist and amateur poet William Hayley (1745–1820), who supported him over the next few years by commissioning illustrations for his own works. The broadside poem Little Tom the Sailor *was the first of these collaborations. As the colophon explains, it was realized to benefit Mrs. Spicer of the neighboring port of Folkestone, who after the death of her husband had been forced to enlist her elder son as a sailor. The lower illustration shows her leaving her two younger children to the care of the ten-year-old Tom as she goes to visit her dying husband in the hospital. It is not clear whether little Tom had actually died in a shipwreck by the time Hayley's somewhat clumsy ballad was written. The headpiece shows him—as depicted in the poem—riding the storm while the spirit of his late father watches over him. We have no account of how many copies of the broadside were printed by Catherine, Blake's wife, on their hand-press. Nine are currently recorded; this one, which surfaced only recently, was probably hand-colored by Blake himself.*

22 Rowlandson

Thomas Rowlandson. A tavern brawl. Original pen-and-ink and watercolor drawing, n.d.

The lively scene is characteristic of the art of Thomas Rowlandson (1756–1827), the greatest caricaturist of his age, most of whose career took place before 1782. As a watercolorist, Rowlandson is also renowned for his graceful plein air scenes, which inspired Sendak, especially for his illustrations to Frank Stockton's The Bee-Man of Orn.

23 The Brothers Grimm

Jakob and Wilhelm Karl Grimm. *Kinder- und Haus-Märchen. Gesammelt durch die Brüder Grimm.* Berlin: G. Reimer, 1819–22.

Jakob and Wilhelm Karl Grimm. *German Popular Stories, translated from the Kinder und Haus Marchen (sic), collected by M.M. Grimm, from oral tradition.* London: Published by C. Baldwyn, Newgate Street, 1823–26.

Jakob and Wilhelm Karl Grimm. *Kinder- und Haus-Märchen. Gesammelt durch die Brüder Grimm. Kleine Ausg.* Berlin: G. Reimer, 1825.

23
Ludwig Grimm. Illustration for "Hänsel und Gretel," from *Kinder- und Haus-Märchen*, 1825.

At the end of the first decade of the nineteenth century, the librarian Jakob Grimm (1785–1863) and his younger brother and fellow librarian Wilhelm (1786–1859) started collecting from a variety of oral sources traditional German folk tales, which they rewrote and published in two volumes in 1812–14 under the title Kinder- und Haus-Märchen. *A much enlarged second edition (comprising more than 200 tales) followed in 1819–22. Its second volume has a frontispiece by Ludwig Grimm (younger brother of the authors) showing Katherina Viehmann, who provided Wilhelm and Jakob with many of their stories, and who in turn is featured in Sendak's illustration to "The Devil and his Three Golden Hairs" in* The Juniper Tree. *George Cruikshank (1792–1878), one of the finest draughtsmen of the first half of the nineteenth century, was the Grimms' first English illustrator and the brothers much admired his work in the 1823–26 London edition of the tales. Ludwig Grimm himself contributed illustrations to the 1825 edition, which influenced Sendak's own work for* The Juniper Tree, *as can be seen from the illustration for "Hansel and Gretel."*

28 SENDAK AT THE ROSENBACH

23
Ludwig Grimm. Title page and frontispiece portrait of Katherina Viehmann, from *Kinder- und Haus-Märchen*, 1819–22.

George Cruikshank. Illustration for the Brothers Grimm's *German Popular Stories*, 1823–26.

22
Rowlandson. A tavern brawl.

27
Caldecott. A foxhunter and his servant.

DUMMIES

7
Top, "Where the Wild Horses Are," 1955.

5
Center opposite, Mr. Rabbit and the Lovely Present.

4
Opposite below, The Moon Jumpers.

7
Directly above, Where the Wild Things Are, 1963.

24 Samuel Palmer

Samuel Palmer. "The Lonely Tower." Etching. [ca. 1870]

Born in 1805, Samuel Palmer was the first among a group of young artists (others being Edward Calvert and George Richmond) who surrounded William Blake in the last three years of his life. It was Blake's friend John Linnell who introduced Palmer to him in 1824, at the time he was working on his Dante illustrations. Later, Palmer married Linnell's daughter Hannah. Trained as a painter and a watercolorist, he only came to the genre of etching in the 1850s. One of the most evocative works of his later period, "The Lonely Tower" was engraved after an 1868 watercolor (now in the Yale Center for British Art) to illustrate lines 85–88 of Milton's poem "Il Penseroso."

> . . . or let my lamp at midnight hour
> Be seen in some lonely tow'r
> Where I may oft outwatch the Bear
> With thrice great Hermes. . .

It was part of an abortive project to illustrate an edition of Milton's shorter poems. Palmer died in 1881.

25 Arthur Hughes

George MacDonald. *At the Back of the North Wind*. With illustrations by Arthur Hughes. New York: George Routledge & Sons, 1871.

Born in London in 1832, Arthur Hughes joined the Pre-Raphaelite movement as early as 1850. In 1857, his friend Dante Gabriel Rossetti invited him to work with him, as well as with Edward Burne-Jones and William Morris, on the decoration of the debating room of the Oxford Union. As a book illustrator, he is best remembered for his collaboration with George MacDonald, especially the collection Dealing with the Fairies *(1867) and* At the Back of the North Wind *(1871). The latter novel is the story—a story in which the author himself appears—of a little boy named Diamond and his involvement with the North Wind fairy. It is illustrated with 75 woodcut vignettes by Hughes. Twenty-four of them had appeared in 1869 in the magazine* Good Words for the Young, *founded in 1869 by Norman Macleod, whom MacDonald himself succeeded as editor. Hughes also illustrated books by MacDonald's children. He died in 1915.*

26 George Pinwell

George Pinwell. "A Milking Song." Proof of wood engraving for *A Round of Days*, 1866.

George Pinwell. "The Goose." Proof of wood engraving for *Wayside Posies*, 1867.

Wayside Posies: Original Poems of the Country Life. Edited by Robert Buchanan. Pictures by G.J. Pinwell, J.W. North, and Frederick Walker. Engraved by the Brothers Dalziel. London: George Routledge and Sons, 1867.

Born in 1842 in Wycombe, near London, George John Pinwell, who died of a pulmonary disease at the age of 33, was one of the most gifted, prolific, and original artists of his generation. Although he was also a painter in oils and watercolors, he was most admired for his book illustrations, such as the ones he realized in 1865 for the works of Oliver Goldsmith. Like those of many other artists of the time, his wood engravings were printed by George, Edward, and Thomas Dalziel, the three brothers from Northumberland who produced some of the greatest Victorian illustrated books (including Alice in Wonderland *and* Alice Through the Looking-Glass). Wayside Posies, *a popular anthology of 37 poems, with 42 illustrations (18 by Pinwell), opens with a full-page woodcut to accompany the poem "The Shadow." Also known as "The Calf," or "The Unwilling Playmate," it displays both Pinwell's craftsmanship and exquisite visual imagination at their most enchanting.*

31
Mozart. *The Magic Flute.* Poster for the Houston Grand Opera production, 1980.

352   AT THE BACK OF THE NORTH WIND.

caught up the little boy, and they ran for the cottage. Jim vanished with a double shuffle, and I went into the house.

When I came out again to return home, the clouds were gone, and the evening sky glimmered through the trees, blue,

and pale-green towards the west, I turned my steps a little aside to look at the stricken beech. I saw the bough torn from the stem, and that was all the twilight would allow me to see. While I stood gazing, down from the sky came a sound of singing, but the voice was neither of lark nor of nightingale: it

25
Arthur Hughes. Diamond in his airy nest.
Illustration for MacDonald's *At the Back of the North Wind*.

26
George Pinwell. "A Milking Song,"
from *A Round of Days;*
"The Calf," from *Wayside Posies;*
"The Goose," from *Wayside Posies.*

28
Melville.
Memorandum of agreement
for the publication of *Pierre*,
1852.

27 Caldecott

Randolph Caldecott. A foxhunter and his servant seen from the back. Original pen-and-ink and watercolor drawing, signed R.C., n.d.

Despite his short, 14-year career, Randolph Caldecott can be considered not only the most original and influential illustrator of his day, but also the true creator of the modern picture book, as evidenced by Hey Diddle Diddle *and* Baby Bunting. *Born in Chester in 1846, he collaborated on several magazines, notably* Punch *and the illustrated* Graphic. *In 1886, he sailed to America on the advice of his doctor, but his health deteriorated and he died in St. Augustine on his arrival in Florida.* "Caldecott," Sendak has written, "is an illustrator, he is a songwriter, he is a choreographer, he is a stage manager, he is a decorator, he is a theater person; he's superb, simply."

36 SENDAK AT THE ROSENBACH

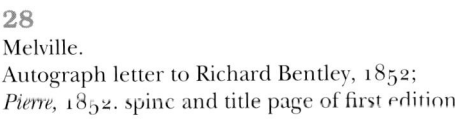

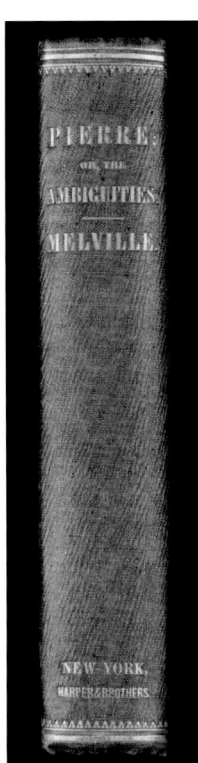

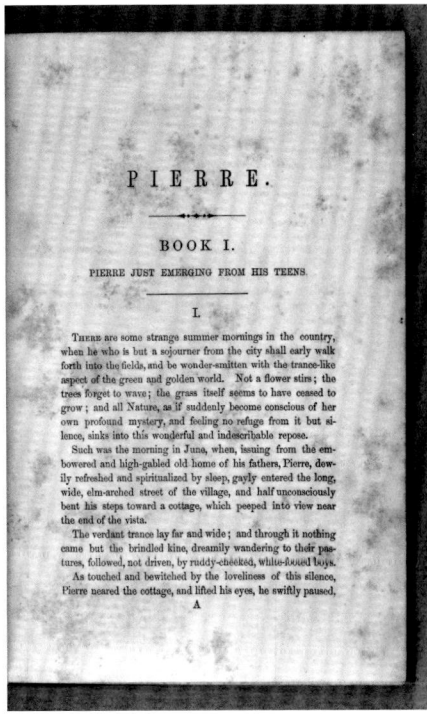

28
Melville.
Autograph letter to Richard Bentley, 1852;
Pierre, 1852. spine and title page of first edition.

28 Melville

Herman Melville. *Pierre; or, The Ambiguities*. New York: Harper & Brothers, 1852. The Edward Stuart Leslie-H. Bradley Martin copy.

Manuscript memorandum of agreement between Harper & Brothers and Herman Melville concerning the publication of *Pierre*, signed by Allan Melville on behalf on his brother. New York, 20 February 1852.

Autograph letter, signed, to Richard Bentley. New York, 16 April, 1852.

Pierre, *Melville's seventh novel, was written at Arrowhead, the farm he had purchased in 1850 in Pittsfield, Massachusetts (his friend Nathaniel Hawthorne lived nearby in Lenox). The publication contract with Harper & Brothers was signed by Allan, Melville's younger brother, who regularly acted as*

29
Beatrix Potter. Three bats.

his agent. The New York firm had previously published *Omoo, Mardi, Redburn, White-Jacket,* and, in the fall of *1851,* Moby-Dick. Richard Bentley had been Melville's English publisher for the last four. The letter Melville wrote to him on April 16, 1852 is the only known one in which he discusses his new novel. It was written in response to a contract proposal from Bentley, who offered Melville a share of half the future profits rather than an advance payment. "Your statement touching my previous book," Melville concedes (the book is The Whale, as Moby-Dick appeared in England), "[does] not, certainly, look very favorably for the profit side of your account." But he then rejects Bentley's proposed terms. "My new book," he argues, "[possesses] unquestionable novelty, as regards my former ones,—treating of utterly new scenes & characters;—and, as I beleive [sic], very much more calculated for popularity than anything you have yet published of mine—being a regular romance, with a mysterious plot to it, & stirring passions at work, and withall, representing a new & elevated aspect of American life..." In the first post-scriptum, he offers to delay American publication of the novel until an agreement is reached in London. In the second post-scriptum, he suggests publishing the book pseudonymously ("By a Vermonter say," and a footnote adds: "or by Guy Winthrop"). In any event, Bentley refused Melville's offer. Pierre appeared in New York in August 1852; the first English edition was published in November from sheets printed in America by Sampson, Low, Son, and Company, Harper's London agent. The sales were mediocre, and the following year part of the first American edition was destroyed in a fire at Harper & Brothers.

29 Beatrix Potter

Beatrix Potter. Studies of bats. Three watercolor drawings on paper. [1885–87?]

These beautiful examples of Beatrix Potter's craftsmanship predate by about fifteen years her great creative period, when she produced, in barely a decade, a series of no fewer than 19 little books for children, triumphantly launched in 1902 with The Tale of Peter Rabbit. Her marriage in 1913 brought her artistic career to an end. Totally self-trained, even though clearly influenced by Caldecott, she rejected to her dying day any suggestion that she could be compared to the the great masters of the past whom she admired, such as Bewick or Constable. An artist of genius, she never considered herself anything but a gifted amateur.

30
William Nicholson.
"The Learned Pig,"
from *The Square Book of Animals*.

30 William Nicholson

William Nicholson. "The Learned Pig."
Lithographic reproduction of a hand-colored
woodcut (proof) for *The Square Book of Animals*
(London: William Heinemann, 1900 [i.e. 1899])

Together with his Swiss contemporary Félix Valloton (another artist much admired by Sendak), William Nicholson (1872–1949) was one of the great masters of the woodcut at the turn of the century. His famous illustrated Alphabet *was published in 1897. Two years later, he produced this series of twelve vignettes of familiar animals. Rudyard Kipling, originally commissioned to write the accompanying verses, withdrew, and the book came out with rhymes by the journalist and critic Arthur Waugh (father of Evelyn and Alec). William Nicholson also designed the costumes for the first production of J.M. Barrie's* Peter Pan *in 1904.*

III
Sendak and Music and the Musical Theater

31 Mozart

The Magic Flute. Original pen-and-ink and tempera drawing for poster for the Houston Grand Opera, ca. 1980.

"All of my pictures are created against a background of music," Sendak writes in the essay which opens the collection Caldecott & Co. *Of all composers, Mozart is the one he cherishes most and who has had the deepest influence on his creative output. He figures twice in person in the books (in* Outside Over There *and* Dear Mili*) and his spirit can be said to permeate Sendak's entire oeuvre, from the early Ruth Krauss books to the double-page dream scene of* Fly by Night. *Even Max in his palm grove seems to inhabit a world akin to that of* The Magic Flute, *and it is no wonder that one of Sendak's earliest encounters with the world of music theater was as designer of a production of this opera for the Houston Grand Opera in 1980, followed by a production of* Idomeneo *in Los Angeles in 1990.*

32 Mahler

Original pen-and-ink and tempera drawing for cover of RCA LP recording of Gustav Mahler's Symphony No. 3 in D minor, 1976.

"The whole of nature finds a voice in it and speaks of something deeply mysterious, something not even guessed at, except perhaps in dreams!" So wrote Gustav Mahler of his third symphony, his longest and most ambitious, written in 1895 and 1896 at Steinbach in the Salzkammergut. Inspired both by Nietzsche's Fröhliche Wissenschaft *and by the world of Arnim and Brentano's* Des Knaben Wunderhorn, *it comprises a long introduction, which evokes Pan's awakening, and six movements. Mahler is another composer with whom Sendak feels a deep spiritual affinity. His illustration for the recording by the Chicago Symphony Orchestra conducted by James Levine seems inspired, in particular, by the third movement, which Mahler originally entitled "What the animals of the forest tell me." It shows Mahler being presented a bouquet of roses by an angel while he is composing in his summer pavilion in the Austrian Alps; in the foreground are animal musicians, one playing the posthorn, which is heard so hauntingly at the end of the movement*

33 Janáček

Maquette of set for Act II, scene 2 for the New York City Opera production of *The Cunning Little Vixen*, ca. 1981.

Original pen-and-ink and tempera drawing for the poster for *The Cunning Little Vixen* at the New York City Opera, ca. 1981.

The penultimate opera written by Leos Janáček (1854–1928), The Cunning Little Vixen *was adapted from a story by the journalist Rudolf Těsnohlídek to illustrate sketches by the Moravian artist Stanislav Lolek. Serialized in the Brno daily* Lidové Noviny (People's News) *in the spring of 1920, it was immensely successful and appeared in book form the following year. Janáček himself wrote the libretto in 1922. The music was completed in January 1924 and the opera,* Prihody Lisky Bytrousky *(literally* The Adventures of the Vixen Sharp-Ears) *was premiered in Brno in November of the same year. Its nine scenes alternate between the animal world and the life of the villagers. Like Mahler in his third symphony, Janáček conceived his work both as a pantheistic hymn to nature and as a moving picture of common humanity.*

34 Really Rosie

Original pen-and-ink and tempera drawing for poster for production of *Really Rosie* at the Chelsea Theater Center, New York, 1980.

In the mid-1970s, Sendak received the commission for an animated film. For the scenario he combined the four books of the 1962 Nutshell Library (Alligators All Around, Chicken Soup with Rice, One Was Johnny, Pierre), using as the narrative frame The Sign on Rosie's Door *(1958), his third book and a personal favorite among his early ones (its origins actually going back to a 1949 project). The result,* Really Rosie, Starring the Nutshell Kids, *was set to music by the rock composer Carole King and was first aired on CBS in 1975. It was later revised into a stage musical, which was premiered in 1980, with sets and costumes designed by Sendak.*

33
Janáček. *The Cunning Little Vixen.*
Maquette of set for Act II, scene 2,
and poster for the New York City Opera production, 1981.

Chronology

1928   Born in Brooklyn, N.Y. to a Jewish family immigrated from Poland before Word War I

1946   Graduates from Lafayette High School

1947   Illustrates physics textbook *Atomics for the Millions*

1948   Enrolls at the Art Students League

1950   Through Ursula Nordstrom, children's book editor at Harper & Brothers, receives commission to illustrate Marcel Aymé's *The Wonderful Farm*, published the following year

1952   Publication of *A Hole Is to Dig* by Ruth Krauss

1953   Visits Europe for the first time

1956   Publication of his first book, *Kenny's Window*

1957   *Very Far Away*, his second book

1960   Publication of *The Sign on Rosie's Door*, his third book, originally conceived in 1949

1962   Publication of the *Nutshell Library* quartet: *Alligators All Around*, *Chicken Soup with Rice*, *One Was Johnny*, *Pierre*

1963   Publication of *Where the Wild Things Are*

1964   Receives the Caldecott Medal, awarded to "the most distinguished American picture book," for *Where the Wild Things Are*

1967   Deposits his archive at the The Philip H. & A.S.W. Rosenbach Foundation; publication of *Higglety Pigglety Pop!*; death of dog Jennie; suffers a serious heart attack while in England on a book tour

1970   Publication of *In the Night Kitchen*; receives the Hans Christian Andersen Medal for his entire oeuvre

1971   Trip to Germany to gather inspiration for the Grimm illustrations; teaches at Yale School of Art

1972   Settles in Ridgefield, Connecticut

1973   Publication of *The Juniper Tree and Other Tales from Grimm;* starts teaching at Parsons School of Design in New York

1975   Animated film *Really Rosie, Starring the Nutshell Kids*, music by Carole King, televised on CBS

1980   Designs sets and costumes for Mozart's *Magic Flute* at Houston Grand Opera; opera *Where the Wild Things Are* premiered at the Théâtre de la Monnaie in Brussels; musical *Really Rosie* opens at the Chelsea Theater in New York

1981   *Outside Over There*

1981   Designs sets and costumes for Janáček's *The Cunning Little Vixen* at the New York City Opera

1982   *The Love for Three Oranges*, by Prokofiev, at the Glyndebourne Opera Festival

1983   *The Nutcracker* for the Pacific Northwest Ballet

1984   Premiere of opera *Higglety Pigglety Pop!* at Glyndebourne

1986   Stravinsky's *Renard* at the Netherlands Opera in Amsterdam

1987   Mozart's *L'oca del Cairo* (originally produced in Kansas City) and *Where the Wild Things Are* as a double-bill at the New York City Opera

1988   Ravel's *L'heure espagnole* and *L'enfant et les sortilèges* at Glyndebourne; publication of *Dear Mili*

1990   Creation of children's theater company The Night Kitchen; Mozart's *Idomeneo* at the Los Angeles Music Center

1993   *We Are All in the Dumps with Jack and Guy*

1995   Illustrates *Pierre* by Herman Melville

Bibliography

Atomics for the Millions by Maxwell Leigh Eidinoff and Hyman Ruchlis. New York: McGraw Hill, 1947.

The Wonderful Farm by Marcel Aymé, translated by Norman Denny. New York: Harper & Brothers, 1951.

Good Shabbos, Everybody by Robert Garvey. [New York] United Synagogue Commission for Jewish Education, 1951.

A Hole Is to Dig by Ruth Krauss. New York: Harper & Brothers, 1952.

Maggie Rose: Her Birthday Christmas by Ruth Sawyer. New York: Harper & Brothers, 1952.

Shadrach by Meindert DeJong. New York: Harper & Brothers, 1953.

Hurry Home, Candy by Meindert DeJong. New York: Harper & Brothers, 1953.

A Very Special House by Ruth Krauss. New York: Harper & Brothers, 1953.

The Giant Story by Beatrice Shenk de Regnier. New York: Harper & Brothers, 1953.

The Magic Pictures: More about the Wonderful Farm by Marcel Aymé, translated by Norman Denny. New York: Harper & Brothers, 1954.

The Wheel on the School by Meindert DeJong. New York: Harper & Brothers, 1954.

I'll Be You and You Be Me by Ruth Krauss. New York: Harper & Brothers, 1954.

Mrs. Piggle-Wiggle's Farm by Betty MacDonald. Philadelphia: The J.B. Lippincott Company, 1954.

The Tin Fiddle by Edward Tripp. New York: Oxford University Press, 1954.

Seven Little Stories on Big Subjects by Gladys Baker Bond. New York: The Anti-Defamation League, B'nai B'rith, 1955.

Happy Hanukah, Everybody by Hyman and Alice Chanover. [New York] United Synagogue Commission for Jewish Education, 1955.

The Little Cow and the Turtle by Meindert DeJong. New York: Harper & Brothers, 1955.

Charlotte and the White Horse by Ruth Krauss. New York: Harper & Brothers, 1955.

What Can You Do with a Shoe? by Beatrice Shenk de Regnier. New York: Harper & Brothers, 1955.

Singing Family of the Cumberlands by Jean Ritchie. New York: Oxford University Press, 1955.

The House of Sixty Fathers by Meindert DeJong. New York: Harper & Brothers, 1956.

I Want to Paint My Bathroom Blue by Ruth Krauss. New York: Harper & Brothers, 1956.

Kenny's Window by Maurice Sendak. New York: Harper & Brothers, 1956.

The Happy Rain by Jack Sendak. New York: Harper & Brothers, 1956.

The Birthday Party by Ruth Krauss. New York: Harper & Brothers, 1957.

Little Bear by Else Holmelund Minarik. New York: Harper & Brothers, 1957.

Circus Girl by Jack Sendak. New York: Harper & Brothers, 1957.

Very Far Away by Maurice Sendak. New York: Harper & Brothers, 1957.

You Can't Get There from Here by Ogden Nash. Boston: Little, Brown, & Company, 1957.

Along Came a Dog by Meindert DeJong. New York: Harper & Brothers, 1958.

Somebody Else's Nut Tree and Other Tales from Children by Ruth Krauss. New York: Harper & Brothers, 1958.

What Do You Say, Dear? by Sesyle Joslin. New York: William R. Scott, 1958.

No Fighting, No Biting! by Else Holmelund Minarik. New York: Harper & Brothers, 1958.

Seven Tales by Hans Christian Andersen. New York: Harper & Brothers, 1959.

Father Bear Comes Home by Else Holmelund Minarik. New York: Harper & Brothers, 1959.

The Moon Jumpers by Janice May Udry. New York: Harper & Row, 1959.

The Acrobat by Maurice Sendak. Privately printed at the Capricorn Press, 1959.

Dwarf Long-Nose by Wilhelm Hauff, translated by Doris Orgel. New York: Random House, 1960.

Open House for Butterflies by Ruth Krauss. New York: Harper & Brothers, 1960.

Little Bear's Friend by Else Holmelund Minarik. New York: Harper & Brothers, 1960.

The Sign on Rosie's Door by Maurice Sendak. New York: Harper & Brothers, 1960.

The Tale of Gockel, Hinkel, and Gackeliah by Clemens Brentano, translated by Doris Orgel. New York: Random House, 1961.

What Do You Do, Dear? by Sesyle Joslin. New York: William R. Scott, 1961.

Let's Be Enemies by Janice May Udry. New York: Harper & Brothers, 1961.

Little Bear's Visit by Else Holmelund Minarik. New York: Harper & Brothers, 1961.

Schoolmaster Whackwell's Wonderful Sons by Clemens Brentano, translated by Doris Orgel. New York: Random House, 1962.

The Singing Hill by Meindert DeJong. New York: Harper & Row, 1962.

The Big Green Book by Robert Graves. [New York] Crowell-Collier Press, 1962.

Nutshell Library: Alligators All Around, Chicken Soup with Rice, One Was Johnny, Pierre by Maurice Sendak. [New York] Harper & Row, 1962.

Mr. Rabbit and the Lovely Present by Charlotte Solotow. New York: Harper & Row, 1962.

Pencil, Pen & Brush Drawing for Beginners by Harvey Weiss. New York: William R. Scott, Inc. [1963].

She Loves Me, She Loves Me Not by Robert Keeshan. New York: Harper & Row, 1963.

Sarah's Room by Doris Orgel. New York: Harper & Row, 1963.

The Griffin and the Minor Canon by Frank Stockton. New York: Holt, Rinehart and Winston, 1963.

Nikolenka's Childhood by Leo Tolstoy, translated by Louise and Aylmer Maude. New York: Pantheon, 1963.

How Little Lori Visited Times Square by Amos Vogel. New York: Harper & Row, 1963.

Where the Wild Things Are by Maurice Sendak. [New York] Harper & Row, 1963.

The Bat-Poet by Randall Jarrell. New York and London: Macmillan, 1964.

The Bee-Man of Orn by Frank Stockton. New York: Holt, Rinehart & Winston, 1964.

Pleasant Fieldmouse by Jan Wahl. New York: Harper & Row, 1964.

Lullabies and Night Songs, edited by William Engvick, music by Alec Wilder. New York: Harper & Row, 1965.

The Animal Family by Randall Jarrell. [New York] Pantheon, 1965.

Hector Protector and *As I Went over the Water* by Maurice Sendak. New York: Harper & Row, 1965.

Zlateh the Goat and Other Stories by Isaac Bashevis Singer. Translated by the author and Elizabeth Shub. [New York] Harper & Row, 1966.

The Aliveness of Peter Rabbit by Maurice Sendak in: *Beatrix Potter: A Centennial Tribute, 1866–1943*. Hartford, CT: The Columbiad Club, 1966.

The Golden Key by George MacDonald. New York: Farrar, Straus & Giroux, 1967.

Higglety Pigglety Pop! or There Must Be More to Life by Maurice Sendak. New York: Harper & Row, 1967.

Poems from William Blake's "Songs of Innocence." London: The Bodley Head, 1967.

Randall Jarrell, edited by Robert Lowell, Peter Taylor, and Robert Penn Warren. New York: Farrar, Straus & Giroux, 1967.

A Kiss for Little Bear by Else Holmelund Minarik. New York: Harper & Row, 1968.

The Light Princess by George MacDonald. New York: Farrar, Straus & Giroux, 1969.

Fantasy Sketches by Maurice Sendak. Philadelphia: The Philip H. & A.S.W. Rosenbach Foundation, 1970.

In the Night Kitchen by Maurice Sendak. [New York] Harper & Row, 1970.

Ten Little Rabbits: A Counting Book with Mino the Magician by Maurice Sendak. [Philadelphia: The Philip H. & A.S.W. Rosenbach Foundation] 1971.

Down the Rabbit Hole by Selma G. Lanes. New York: Atheneum, 1971.

Pictures by Maurice Sendak. New York: Harper & Row, 1971.

The Art of Claud Lovat Fraser by Clive E. Driver. Philadelphia: The Philip H. & A.S.W. Rosenbach Foundation, 1971 [includes a tribute by Sendak].

The Juniper Tree and Other Tales from Grimm. Translated by Lore Segal and Randall Jarrell. New York: Farrar, Straus & Giroux, 1973.

King Grisly-Beard: A Tale from the Brothers Grimm. Translated by Edgar Taylor. New York: Farrar, Straus & Giroux, 1973.

Fortunia by Mme d'Aulnoy, translated by Richard Schaubeck. Privately printed, 1974.

The Maxfield Parrish Poster Book, with an introduction by Maurice Sendak. New York: Harmony Books, 1974.

The Complete Fairy Tales and Stories by Hans Christian Andersen, translated by Erik Christian Haugaard. Garden City, N.Y.: Doubleday & Company, 1974.

Really Rosie, Starring the Nutshell Kids. Scenario, lyrics and pictures by Maurice Sendak, music by Carole King, design by Jane Byers Bierhorst. New York: Harper & Row, 1975.

Beyond the Bedroom Wall: A Family Album by Larry Woiwode. New York: Farrar, Straus & Giroux, 1975.

Die Geschichte von den sieben kleinen Riesen by Maurice Sendak. Zurich: Diogenes Verlag, 1975.

Little Nemo by Winsor McCay. New York: Nostalgia Press, 1976 [includes a review by Maurice Sendak].

Fly by Night by Randall Jarrell. New York: Farrar, Straus & Giroux, 1976.

Some Swell Pup, or Are You Sure You Want a Dog? by Maurice Sendak and Matthew Margolis. New York: Farrar, Straus & Giroux, 1976.

Seven Little Monsters by Maurice Sendak. New York: Harper & Row, 1977.

The Portent by George MacDonald. San Francisco: Harper & Row, 1979.

Outside Over There by Maurice Sendak. [New York] Harper & Row, 1981.

Victorian Color Picture Books, edited by Jonathan Cott. Commentary by Maurice Sendak. New York: Stonehill Publishing, 1983.

The Love for Three Oranges: The Glyndebourne Version by Frank Corsaro. Stage and Costume Designs [by] Maurice Sendak. New York: Farrar, Straus & Giroux, 1984.

Nutcracker by E.T.A. Hoffmann, translated by Ralph Manheim. New York: Crown Publishers, 1984.

The Cunning Little Vixen by Rudolf Tésnohlídek, translated by Tatiana Firkusny, Maritza Morgan and Robert T. Jones, with an afterword by Robert T. Jones. New York: Farrar, Straus & Giroux, 1985.

In Grandpa's House by Philip Sendak. Translated and adapted by Seymour Barofsky. New York: Harper & Row, 1985.

The Lost World by Randall Jarrell. New York: Macmillan, 1985.

Posters by Maurice Sendak. New York: Harmony Books, Crown Publishers, 1986.

Caldecott & Co.: Notes on Books & Pictures by Maurice Sendak. New York: Farrar, Straus & Giroux, 1988.

Dear Mili by Wilhelm Grimm. Translated by Ralph Manheim. New York: Farrar, Straus & Giroux, 1988.

The Children's Books of Randall Jarrell by Jerome Griswold. Introduction by Mary Jarrell. Athens: University of Georgia Press, 1988.

I Saw Esau: The Schoolchild's Pocket-Book, edited by Iona and Peter Opie. London: Walker Books, 1992.

We Are All in the Dumps with Jack and Guy by Maurice Sendak. New York: HarperCollins, 1993.

Pierre; or, The Ambiguities by Herman Melville. New York: HarperCollins, 1995.

Reference Works

Lanes, Selma G. *The Art of Maurice Sendak.* New York: Harry N. Abrams, 1980.

Harnahan, Joyce Y. *Works of Maurice Sendak 1947–1994: A Collection with Comments.* Portsmouth, N.H.: Peter E. Randall Publisher, 1995.

Catalogue Copyright © 1995 by The Rosenbach Museum and Library.

Jacket front: Copyright © 1976 by Maurice Sendak.

Jacket back: Copyright © 1980 by Maurice Sendak.

Page 4: Illustration from the book *The Moon Jumpers* copyright © 1959 by Maurice Sendak. Published by HarperCollins.

Page 6: Illustration from the book *The Golden Key* copyright © 1967 by Maurice Sendak. Published by Farrar, Straus & Giroux.

Page 9: Illustration from the book *Mr. Rabbit and the Lovely Present* copyright © 1962 by Maurice Sendak. Published by HarperCollins.

Page 10: Illustration from the book *The Bee-Man of Orn* copyright © 1964 by Maurice Sendak. Published by HarperCollins.

Page 11, top: Illustration from the book dummy for *The Griffin and the Minor Canon* copyright © 1963 by Maurice Sendak.

Page 11, bottom: Illustration from the book *The Bee-Man of Orn* copyright © 1964 by Maurice Sendak. Published by HarperCollins.

Page 12: Illustrations from the book *The Bat Poet* copyright © 1964 by Maurice Sendak. Published by Macmillan Publishing Company.

Page 13: Illustrations from the book *Zlateh the Goat* copyright © 1966 by Maurice Sendak. Published by HarperCollins.

Pages 14 and 15: Illustrations from the book *Where the Wild Things Are* copyright © 1963 by Maurice Sendak. Published by HarperCollins.

Page 16: Illustration from the book *Higglety Pigglety Pop!* copyright © 1967 by Maurice Sendak. Published by HarperCollins.

Page 17, top: Illustrations from the book *Higglety Pigglety Pop!* copyright © 1967 by Maurice Sendak. Published by HarperCollins.

Page 17, bottom: Illustration from the book *The Golden Key* copyright © 1967 by Maurice Sendak. Published by Farrar, Straus & Giroux.

Page 18: Illustration from the book *The Light Princess* copyright © 1969 by Maurice Sendak. Published by Farrar, Straus & Giroux.

Page 19, top: Illustration from the book *The Light Princess* copyright © 1969 by Maurice Sendak. Published by Farrar, Straus & Giroux.

Page 19, bottom: Illustration from the book *In the Night Kitchen* copyright © 1970 by Maurice Sendak. Published by HarperCollins.

Pages 20 and 21: Illustrations from the book *The Juniper Tree* copyright © 1973 by Maurice Sendak. Published by Farrar, Straus & Giroux.

Page 22: Illustrations from the book *Outside Over There* copyright © 1981 by Maurice Sendak. Published by HarperCollins.

Page 23: Illustrations from the book *We Are All in the Dumps with Jack and Guy* copyright © 1993 by Maurice Sendak. Published by Michael diCapua Books, HarperCollins Publishers.

Page 24: Illustration from the book *Fly by Night* copyright © 1976 by Maurice Sendak. Published by Farrar, Straus & Giroux.

Page 25, top: Illustration from the book *Fly by Night* copyright © 1976 by Maurice Sendak. Published by Farrar, Straus & Giroux.

Page 25, bottom: Preliminary study for *Outside Over There* copyright © 1981 by Maurice Sendak. *Outside Over There* published by HarperCollins.

Page 26: Illustration from the book *Dear Mili* copyright © 1988 by Maurice Sendak. Published by Farrar, Straus & Giroux.

Pages 30 and 31, across top: Dummy for *Where the Wild Horses Are* copyright © 1955 by Maurice Sendak.

Page 30, center; Dummy for *Mr. Rabbit and the Lovely Present* copyright © 1962 by Maurice Sendak.

Page 30, bottom: Dummy for *The Moon Jumpers* copyright © 1959 by Maurice Sendak.

Page 31, bottom: Dummy for *Where the Wild Things Are* copyright © 1963 by Maurice Sendak.

Page 33: copyright © 1980 by Maurice Sendak.

Page 42: Maquette of set for *The Cunning Little Vixen* copyright © 1981 by Maurice Sendak.

Page 43: Copyright © 1981 by Maurice Sendak.

Pictured materials by William Blake, Ludwig Grimm, Thomas Rowlandson, Randolph Caldecott, George Cruikshank, Arthur Hughes, George Pinwell, Herman Melville, Beatrix Potter, and William Nicholson, from the collection of Maurice Sendak.